# Smart Kid Terminology

*Smart Kid Terminology* is your go-to resource for helping gifted and advanced learners identify and work through their feelings, thoughts, and experiences in relevant, accessible terms.

The illustrations and descriptive definitions in this book demystify educational terminology that can often be dense and difficult to understand. Each section features a description, example of the term in action, and a solution with recommendations for practice. Light-hearted and encouraging, this book covers terms like *perfectionist, procrastinator, bored in school, isolation by choice*, and more!

For young learners, this book is a guide for identifying and expressing their feelings. For parents, it provides a tool to help them develop coping strategies together, and for teachers and counselors, it's an essential starting point for understanding the needs and emotions of their most advanced students.

**Brenda Kay Small** is Affiliate Professor of educational leadership at Regis University and an author, presenter, and advocate for Advanced Learners. Find her at www.leadsmarteducation.com.

# SMART KID TERMINOLOGY

## 25 TERMS TO HELP GIFTED LEARNERS SEE THEMSELVES AND FIND SUCCESS

### BRENDA KAY SMALL

Routledge
Taylor & Francis Group

NEW YORK AND LONDON

Cover image: © Getty Images

First published 2022
by Routledge
605 Third Avenue, New York, NY 10158

and by Routledge
4 Park Square, Milton Park, Abingdon, Oxon, OX14 4RN

*Routledge is an imprint of the Taylor & Francis Group, an informa business*

*Library of Congress Cataloging-in-Publication Data*
Names: Small, Brenda Kay, author.
Title: Smart kid terminology : 25 terms to help gifted learners see themselves and
    find success / Brenda Kay Small.
Description: New York, NY : Routledge, 2022. | Includes bibliographical references. |
Identifiers: LCCN 2021048126 (print) | LCCN 2021048127 (ebook) |
    ISBN 9781032189437 (hardback) | ISBN 9781032189277 (paperback) |
    ISBN 9781003257103 (ebook)
Subjects: LCSH: Gifted children—Education. | Gifted children—Psychology. |
    Special education—Terminology.
Classification: LCC LC3957 .S63 2022 (print) | LCC LC3957 (ebook) |
    DDC 371.95—dc23/eng/20211109
LC record available at https://lccn.loc.gov/2021048126
LC ebook record available at https://lccn.loc.gov/2021048127

ISBN: 978-1-032-18943-7 (hbk)
ISBN: 978-1-032-18927-7 (pbk)
ISBN: 978-1-003-25710-3 (ebk)

DOI: 10.4324/9781003257103

Typeset in Futura
by Apex CoVantage, LLC

St. Jude Children's®
Research Hospital

Finding cures. Saving children.
ALSAC • DANNY THOMAS, FOUNDER

# Contents

# Contents

# Contents

# Preface

There is truth in the wisdom that necessity is the catalyst for change and innovations. This book is a result of what I needed in my practice as an educator. It was critical that students, parents, counselors, administrators, and teachers understand what a student is experiencing. As a school leader, I saw a common confusion as I spoke with parents and led conferences. Students described themselves as misfits, so different from others. I needed a tool to help them and let them know they are not different, but beautifully unique and special. There were dense books and brief websites with explanations. There was no resource that I could put in their hands that everyone understood.

Isn't good communication the key to success? The advanced learner is complex, as are all children. If their support systems do not understand them, there will be a disconnect in that support. The child and their advocates need a tool that gives everyone a common language. That language leads to efficient communication and a common understanding.

The book is designed to encourage the reader to peruse the pages looking for that one term that relates to themself or others. It is a simple left-side description and a right-side strategy, plus relevant illustrations. It will not take much time to find the appropriate term in the chapters divided into academic, social, and emotional terms.

To select the terms, I drew from my practical experiences in schools as a teacher, administrator, and consultant. It did not take long to compile a list that was much longer than 25 terms. After consulting research and current practices, the terms were narrowed to 25. These terms are used weekly, if not daily, in my profession. Yes, all high achievers have experienced these terms at some time in their educational and developmental journey. Some students will relate a real-life scenario for each of the 25 terms.

I believe our advanced learners are one of our nation's greatest natural resources. Their minds have the capacity to save our environment, cure diseases, and improve our lives in ways we cannot imagine. Too often, these children are left to fend for themselves in classrooms and homes. Their unique intelligence is not widely understood or explored for individual growth. It is my hope this book will be a part of the solution in creating a common understanding of these precious people.

*Chapter 1*

# Terms, Communication, & Critical Resources

## Learning these terms gives power to positively impact every Smart Kid's future

DOI: 10.4324/9781003257103 - 1

# Seemingly Simple Terms Are Important

Imagine a place where there existed a clear and universal understanding of the words that described Smart Kids and others in their world. In this place, a word or term holds a power to generate good conversations among parents, students, administrators, teachers, counselors, mental health and medical providers, grandparents, and other education advocates. A clear understanding of the term could eliminate the misdiagnosis, miseducation, and misunderstanding of the world of the high-level learner.

Common barriers exist in schools and homes without clear communication.

\* \* \* \* \*

Scenario:

5 people are seated around a conference table: 2 parents, 1 student, 1 counselor, and 1 teacher of the Gifted and Talented. Conversations start like most school conferences. The student is asked why they are not working to their full potential. As the adults question the child, it is obvious there is a lack of understanding of the Smart Kid.

The student is earning top grades in all but one class, has only 2 close friends, is woefully unorganized and thrives on isolation. The student shows frustration with the unhappiness of the adults. Parents and the counselor are equally frustrated and looking for either incentives or punishments to encourage improvement.

The teacher of the Gifted and Talented explains the common academic, social, and emotional traits of Smart Kids with one valuable resource.

\* \* \* \* \*

The frustration in such conferences is the result of the confusion of how students think and feel. There is a void in the communication. Often, student advocates base their own understandings and terroneous definitions on past experiences in education or on the advice of other parents or teachers. Good communication with high level learners starts with common terms used in the exploration of their academic, social, and emotional assets and concerns.

*Smart Kid Terminology* is the resource we imagined that encourages a universal understanding. It is kept handy and used to start conversations and for self-reflection. This resource is essential in the previous scenario. All readers who know and support high-level learners will identify with these terms. The terms include statements and real-life situations from a student perspective. This clear communication with children and education advocates is a pivotal component in making positive life changes.

The easy-to-follow chapters are divided into Academic, Social, and Emotional terms. This division gives the reader an easy opportunity to scan the pages. Clinical and dictionary definitions are not necessary for a student to find themselves in the pages. The current strategies are research based with textbook definitions embedded into the descriptions. More academic definitions are found in the resources.

This book identifies up-to-date terms that are currently used in education circles. The descriptions and quotes are from the real-life experiences of people, students, children, teachers, counselors, parents, and others. Feelings depicted in these quotes are often more relatable than a scientific definition. Each term definition strives to create the emotion felt by the Smart Kid.

Terms are organized in a double-page layout that facilitates an efficient look at the possible problem and the suggested solution. The left side of the page describes the trait as experienced by advanced learners. The right side of the page offers suggestions for coping and managing the trait. Take notice that these traits are often a positive part of the Smart Kid's life. In these situations, the term is used to help describe the trait to the advocates.

The power of a picture! The illustrations are personally relevant in their depiction of the angst and joy of the characters. Such emotional portrayals display what a child may not be able to explain. Identifying with the characters is a part of the learning process. Such self-discovery empowers to improve and manage challenges. The right-side illustrations and suggestions convey a positive reflection of the possibilities for success.

## Who Should Have This Resource?

The quick answer is *"Anyone who wants to learn more about themselves and others."* Such knowledge is powerful. Honest self-reflection when reading the terms brings a feeling of acceptance and community to the Smart Kid. As a resource for advocates, these pages are filled with information to be utilized and shared.

*Students*

Age and grade level are irrelevant when looking through the terms in search of one that applies. Some of the terms occur over the broad spans of time in a student's school career. Others evolve and disappear throughout the formative years.

If you are the student, take a few minutes to flip through the pages one chapter at a time. Select the term which represents the current thoughts and feelings in the Academic, Social, and Emotional chapters. Use the descriptions and quotes to agree and disagree with the trait's portrayal. Talk about why the words are meaningful or what needs to be changed. Check out the illustration. Is the self-reflection there in a clear sense of reality? Take one of the strategies, or maybe two, and work them into the daily life of school and family. Return to the term in a few days or a week. Find another strategy to apply. Return often. Talk about the results. Look for accountability with those who care. Share the terms with friends, family, and trusted teachers. Point out their value and relevance. Keep talking about it.

These terms represent common gifted traits. A reader unfamiliar with giftedness may have concerns when reviewing the complexity of the numerous terms. Being a Smart Kid is not easy. The depth of the highly intelligent mind is beyond the comprehension of most student advocates. A tool is needed to find a common ground in communication and collaboration. Use this resource as a start to conversations about the complexity of the gifted mind.

*Teachers*

A classroom is filled with students with diverse personalities, learning styles, and individual needs. Regardless of how a schedule of classes is built, there are needs in every seat of a teacher's classroom. From advanced academic classes to non-academic classes, teachers can identify students with the traits in this book. By keeping this resource handy in their classroom, it can be used as an example or to open discussions with students. The teachers assigned to Gifted and Talented programs will cherish this resource as a clear and effective communication tool for students and their parents.

Depending on the age level and grouping, teachers will observe how students wander over and pick it up. They like reading about themselves. They may find it difficult to keep from sharing their epiphanies about themselves or others as they identify with the terms. Teachers are encouraged to lend this resource to students during reading time. Ask them to find a term and managing strategies that remind them of themselves.

Communicating opinions and observations to parents about their children can be difficult for teachers. These terms provide a gentle platform to start conversations by building relationships with better informed parents. Teachers may use this tool for parents who are experiencing frustration in a parent conference or have a child who is newly identified as gifted. Parents who are requesting gifted screening for their child can be given this tool. It will provide them with important background knowledge of high-level learner traits. Teachers are encouraged to share with other teachers who may be struggling with advanced learners.

## *Administrators*

Leading a school fills the day of the administrator with critical priorities that directly impact the lives of their students and staff. It is an enormous task to create an environment that meets the needs of each type of learner. Yet, the time spent advising a teacher, participating in a conference, or talking with a parent on the phone is pivotal to the leader's success. These conversations lead to a positive culture with happy parents and students. By learning each term and its strategies, a school leader has a toolbox to pull from to help their students, parents, and teachers.

Administrators of all grade levels and types of schools have copies handy for student interactions and parent conferences. The explanations and examples within the terms help guide conversations in both the academic and discipline circles. Check out copies to families and individual students for further study and application of the strategies. Knowledge of these traits enables the informed administrator to keep an eye on scheduling top level learners. The placement of students into inappropriately grouped classes causes frustration, withdrawal, and feelings of isolation. An astute administrator will break down barriers in the school for their students to thrive at the top of their learning abilities.

Create positive and informative professional development for teaching and support staff using the terms as a curriculum to instruct teachers how to work with all students. Showcase a term at each faculty meeting. For example, provide data on students identified as gifted, yet who are not thriving. Then, use specific terms to start small discussion groups that create strategies to employ schoolwide. Support personnel such as nurses, secretaries, and aids need to learn and apply their knowledge of the traits to better understand and serve families and teachers.

Administrators often receive requests for the acceleration of Smart Kids outside their grade level. As students move through the grade levels, they may select more accelerated programs. Have the terms ready to share and create presentations to educate incoming parents and their students during orientations. This practice can help avoid inappropriate placement of students that can have long-term adverse effects.

## *Counselors*

School counselors reside in each school to serve the needs of students through scheduling, assessing, and even counseling if time allows. They are invaluable assets and called on to complete tasks beyond their scope of available time and even knowledge. The counselor is often the first to know about a student in distress. They are the "safe place to land" for many students in vast and growing schools. Their time is precious, with daunting expectations to know each student and their idiosyncrasies. With this one-stop resource, counselors can review the terms and learn the strategies for efficient and frequent use.

Precious time in a school conference is streamlined by using this resource to explain a trait. A quick look at the term, illustrations, and strategies helps participants focus on positive results. Counselors will keep this resource handy during conferences and phone conversations with concerned parents. Sharing the resources provided for the terms is a great place to start the encouragement of further research. Furthermore, students will browse through the pages in the counselor's office looking for themselves. Such clear communication is critical to helping students thrive.

## *Parents and High-level Learning Adults*

Raising a Smart Kid seems like it would be easy ... to outsiders. Each year of growth brings new challenges. Most are unpredictable, but all are critical to the academic, social, and emotional foundation of a child. The first lesson is to not assume they will thrive on their own because of their intelligence. Parenting is always critical. This resource is a guide for the present and what may occur in a child's life. Find the terms that identify your child. Study the traits, illustrations, and strategies.

These terms are a great conversation starter for any age of child. Ask them to add to the feelings and causes on the left-hand pages. Then, encourage your child to add to the solutions and strategies. What works for them? Talk, debate, and discuss the terms that are relatable.

Parents often identify themselves as gifted adults. Utilize the terms to clarify past feelings and situations. Remember, traits parents find irritating in their own children – such as stubbornness, perfection, worry, excessive questioning, and resistance to interruptions – have a place in adult life as leadership, empathy, curiosity, and perseverance.

Celebrate giftedness in adults with the power of knowing these traits and strategies. Share them with high-level learning adult friends who identify with the traits. Watch as the self-reflection evolves into how to support their own children and apply strategies in their own lives.

## *Advocates of High-level Thinkers*

The knowledge of the traits and strategies of high-level thinkers is valuable outside the school setting. Community members and other businesspersons will find the descriptions enlightening. Hiring managers are required to hire effective and efficient workers. These traits exist in their applicants. Understanding the terms and strategies assists in the decision-making process during hiring. Plus, the traits provide information for cautiously-worded interview questions. Mitigators, salespersons, and lobbyists are just a few professions that need to have knowledge of these traits and strategies.

Even more than that, any profession serving children or adults in need demands the knowledge of these terms. Social workers, shelter operators, foster families, etc. are called to know and serve the nation's most vulnerable people. Becoming familiar with these traits gives one more tool in assisting each person on an individual level. Conversations start when such advocates hand this book to a person with the instructions to "find yourself in these pages." From that point, advocacy accelerates, and lives are changed.

## **Why Is This Resource So Important?**

Knowledge is power, with a strength to entice growth. The life experiences of a child either nurture or deflate their abilities. With a reflection on how unchallenged life experiences can weaken strengths, break spirits, and create negative senses of self, the journey to healing starts. A high-level learner grows when given opportunities in challenging academic, social, and emotional environments.

All students come from unique backgrounds, with pressures or permissions that many of their supporters cannot identify with from their own childhoods. These terms provide a clear meaning that strengthens the articulation of how a child may feel. Advocates are given a common resource to refer to for conversations and explanations. The book is written and illustrated for this purpose.

Good life-learning practices are rewarded with knowing these terms for all levels of learners and ages. So many of these traits are taken for granted or not understood as special. There is no "normal" in any child. The ultimate quest for all student advocates is to encourage giftedness in a welcoming and safe environment. Difficulty occurs when a student or adult unconsciously, or purposefully, hides their giftedness or adapts to fit in at lower levels. Their gifts are lost in a desire to fit in.

The terminology selected is based on the commonality of terms used in gifted conversations in schools and education research institutions. Beyond that, the choice of terms and the scenarios reflects the author's practice as a teacher and administrator. Each is true to life and relevant to the daily life of a high-level learner.

Share this book. It is no good to anyone if it is sitting on a shelf in an office, classroom, or home. Flip through it often. If a person is recognized in a term, share it with them. They may not realize this trait until they read the term, the strategies, and see themselves in the illustrations. Disagree with the definitions and strategies, add personal examples. Just talk about it!

The resources following each chapter are a treasure trove of opportunities for further study and exploration of the terms. Several of the resources are repeated in each chapter. Take a note of these important and reliable publications and citations. Use the resources as a jumping-off point for more research. Recognize the difference between the academic research-based sources and the more opinion-orientated resources. All are effective in a quest for more knowledge.

## Table of Terms: Academic, Social, and Emotional

| Academic | Social | Emotional |
|---|---|---|
| Perfectionist | Isolation by Choice | Intensity |
| SO Unorganized | Frog Pond Theory | Imposter Syndrome |
| Procrastinator | Bored in School | Sensitivity |
| Underachiever | Not Trying That | Strong Sense of Justice |
| Remembering Everything | Already Know This | Depression |
| Experiencing Asynchronicity | Cheaters and Liars | Stress Mastery |
| Chronic Overthinker | Feeling Different | Self-Criticism |
| Multiple Exceptionalities/2e | High Expectations of Others | Gifted Kid Burnout |
| | Does Gifted Always Mean Smart? | |

## Chapter 2

# Smart Kid Academic Terminology

### Terms that impact the Smart Kid's academic & cognitive performance

DOI: 10.4324/9781003257103 - 2

# The Perfectionist

There is NO acceptance of any standard short of perfection. There is no such identity as a "personal best." There is only "The Best."

A constant unhealthy focus on how they compare to others.

Tends to avoid trying something new because perfection takes time.

The Smart Kid's identity may be a part of this personality type as they focus on results and set unrealistic standards. This issue creates a fear of failure.

Achieving perfection as compared to everyone else's abilities is academically and emotionally critical.

Left unchecked, this trait has a strong hold on a person and can lead to low self-esteem and depression.

This trait is often misdiagnosed and misunderstood as laziness, fear, or a lack of understanding.

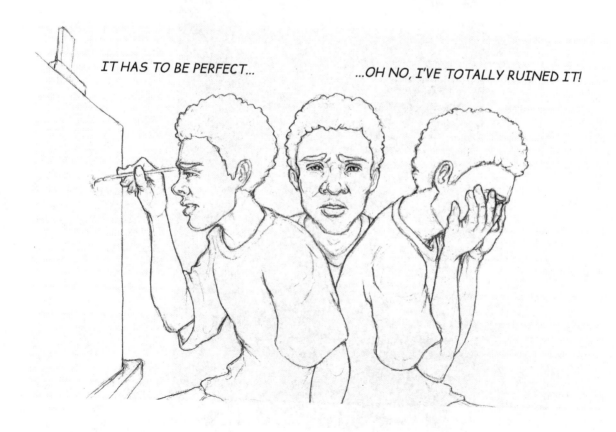

# Managing Perfectionism

*Confront* it! Say the **"P-WORD"** out loud.

When the *perfectionism beast* occurs *feel* and *recognize* the physical changes of anxiety.

*Take a meditative moment* to re-focus and re-evaluate the situation.

*Take a mental walk* through a scene where the outcome is not perfect. Is this result OK? Is it worth this present anxiety?

*Notice* when perfectionism is hindering healthy risk-taking.

*Be aware* when perfectionism is a barrier to intellectual innovation.

*Recognize* this may be an obsessive-compulsive behavior. Seek a rationalization of why it does not need to be perfect.

*Look away* and *walk away*. Leave it alone for a short time and return with a renewed spirit.

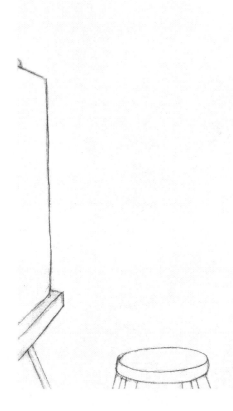

NOT PERFECT, BUT GOOD PRACTICE.

# I Am SO Unorganized

*Keeping order or planning* is not a part of the daily schedule, expectations, or activities.

The question "where is my _____?" occurs almost *hourly*.

When this trait *impacts productivity and results, it creates stress.*

Surrounding people often voice their *frustration* with this person's lost items or inability to remember scheduled events.

There are *missed* deadlines, messy desks, and misplaced assignments.

How can you find anything in that backpack?

*Physical appearance* may not be a priority, resulting in messy hair and clothes.

Often frustrated with rigid systems of organization and accountability.

Often focuses on the *big picture* and is considered a *visionary.*

Has a *lack of understanding* and curiosity about people who spend time organizing their space, backpacks, or write lists.

Considers *organization systems* a waste of time. Let's get right to the work.

# The Organized Unorganized Smart Kid

*Acknowledge* and *recognize* the cost of disorganization. List the past events that were negatively impacted by this trait.

*Write down everything* on a calendar. Everything! Experiment with desk, wall, or digital calendars. Redundancy works. Use all types of calendars until good habits are formed.

*Take detailed notes* during classes or meetings. This activity helps with focus and appeals to the visual and kinesthetic learner.

Check out a person who has a *good organization system.* Watch and learn from them. Observe and ask questions.

*Use technology* often! Enter dates and times for each day. Use alarm reminders.

*Write lists* and keep them close. Keep a list with sound reminders on a cell phone. Color-code and create sub lists. Enjoy the physical task of drawing a line through the completed task. Keep a completed list to celebrate growth.

*Routines* help create a predictable and organized day. Work diligently to stay with the same routine for each school or workday for sleep, meals, meetings, seatwork, and social time.

*Talk to a friend, teacher, or family member* about your plan to stay organized. Ask them to ask to see your calendar or lists on a regular basis. Accountability is essential to stay on track.

# The Procrastinator

*Delaying the completion* of a task for any reason. Ignoring time.

*Ineffective self-motivation* to continue or start anything.

*Making excuses* to perform trivial tasks instead of the important tasks.

Procrastination has a fierce hand on the thinking process, making it a powerful influence on a *"flight or fight"* situation. "Should I run to something else or should I get in there and DO IT!"

A procrastinator may have *too much freedom* to decide their own actions or schedules.

Procrastinators are often perceived as *lazy.* Smart Kids may feel this perception is OK if it can stop people from pushing them.

The world's *unlimited intellectual and informational distractions* feed the procrastination beast.

Taking the *first step* on completing a project is much more difficult than the next ten steps.

# Managing Procrastination Takes Action

*Overcoming procrastination is a skill.* It must be practiced daily.

*Make a list* with times for task completion every morning or before bedtime. The most important tasks are #1, #2 and #3. Keep the list close all day. Give a reward for completion.

Delve deep inside thoughts to *find the real reason for the avoidance* of this task or activity. Once determined, use its power to influence future tasks.

Develop a vision of what is to be completed and a deadline. Walk through this mental exercise daily.

*Willpower is an intrinsic motivation.* Use this *power* to fight any delay with purposeful steps toward completion.

*Multi-tasking breeds procrastination.* Complete one task at a time successfully before moving to the next task.

*Recognize* the procrastination beast when it appears. Call it out! Take action steps to face it down and fight it with a vengeance!

Add others to the completion team. This assembly may be a study group, book club, or a group of people meeting to work independently. All members hold each other accountable to due dates.

# I Am an Underachiever and I Know It

Defined as the difference between a student's performance and *their ability to perform* at a higher academic level.

A *lack of enthusiasm* for learning. Even the past interests are not exciting. New subjects are not considered interesting.

Give frequent *negative references* about themselves, and their abilities to succeed.

Communicating that the reason for trying and doing well is *not valuable to them.*

*Negative attitudes* toward teachers and school. A change from previous school years.

Academic performance *drops slowly* or with a transition into a new grade or school.

A *negative mind shift occurs* where a positive attitude used to be.

Low self-concept leads to an *unwillingness to take academic risks.*

The Smart Kid begins to *seek social isolation* without giving a reason.

*Peer groups change* to associating with lower-achieving students.

# Encouraging Achievement

Keep it Positive! *Identify the root causes* and gently peel back the layers causing the lack of motivation. This will take time. Do not rush the process.

Focus and celebrate the student's gifts and *talents*. Find these successes. They are in every Smart Kid's life.

Find a *worthy mentor* to stay on top of the student's attitude. This person could be anyone from a coach, a friend, another parent, or a counselor.

Listen to the underachiever! It may take *professional counseling* to find the true cause and make changes.

Work diligently to respectfully *strengthen the cooperation between teachers and families.* This may be perceived by a Smart Kid as pushy. Delicately work in positive experiences.

Ensure that every meeting with the underachiever *ends on a positive note.* In addition, there are clear agreed goals with deadlines.

*Find peers with the same strengths* and get together often. These peers may be outside the Smart Kid's age group or grade level.

*Keep lists and reminders* with due dates in a common place in the home. Use a "check off" system to show growth. Work toward reward.

*A new technology* can help poorly developed fine motor skills and organization that may slow down achievement. A new gadget can be a motivator.

# I Remember EVERYTHING!

Advanced learners often have *above average long-term memories.*

A great memory is often the *first clue a young child is gifted.* It is not uncommon for a teenager to remember details from experiences as a toddler.

The intake of information may become *overwhelming.*

Families and friends may become frustrated with an *inability to recall* the same details.

The Smart Kid experiences *frustration with others* who do not remember minuscule or seemingly inconsequential details.

Students may use *self-discovered tools* to enhance their memory and wonder why others cannot do the same.

Peers and teachers may *tire of the Smart Kid's ability to recall* and answer questions quickly and accurately.

There is often a feeling of being different from others, which leads to avoiding contributions to groups.

*WHAT DO THEY MEAN, THEY DON'T REMEMBER?*

# Managing a Great Memory

*Understanding social clues* that indicate verbalizing a memory is not always appropriate.

*Acknowledge* an advanced memory compared to others. Embrace the difference without considering the judgment of others.

*Understand the limitations* of others in conversation. They do not have your depth of understanding due to your amazing recall.

*Intellectually compartmentalize* information for later assessment.

*Reset* the memory of others by describing the details so your conversation will be on an even ground.

*Maintain a pillar of honesty* when recalling facts. A reputation for a great memory might tempt the gifted person to provide facts for their own gain.

Remember, everything can be positive or a tragically negative experience of *past trauma.*

*Past trauma* may remain a raw emotion and necessitate professional counseling.

DO YOU REMEMBER THE PART WHEN...?

# How Am I Experiencing Asynchronicity?

Emotional, intellectual, and physical attributes are *growing at different rates.*

High level skills are not common for this Smart Kid's *chronological age.*

*Finds the same-age peers to be odd* and exhibit puzzling or illogical behaviors.

"My body seems to be out of sync with my brain." Said by a ten-year-old who completes math problems at a college level yet struggles catching a baseball.

May exhibit the *typical emotional and social behavior* of their age group, but with extremely high intelligence.

The realization of being a misfit or feeling out of sync with peers may cause anxiety or depression.

*Parents are often confused* by their child having inconsistent abilities in subjects.

The asynchronous person may experience *impulsiveness and struggles when learning new subjects.*

A *new environment* may bring anxiety and a fear of failure.

Fleeing challenges and *running toward activities and subjects* where success is experienced is common.

MATH COMES SO EASILY...

WHY IS READING SO HARD?

# I Am Multi-talented, and I Am Amazing!

*Growing into Giftedness* takes awareness and patience. Remain optimistic!

Avoid using *age* as the definition of ability. Accept high-level gifts and share them with others.

Encourage working in groups of different ages and types of learners.

Protect social and emotional development from negative influences.

*One size does not fit all!* Embrace differences in skills, development, and abilities.

*Find your people!* There are peers with the same asynchronous experiences.

*Mix it up!* Work and learn with older students. Grow!

Seek intellectual stimulation *outside of the same age group*.

Seek support for the peer and teacher interactions through their education about Asynchronicity.

As adulthood approaches, a more balanced role gradually emerges.

Find a commonality with what the child is good at when exposing the child to new subjects. Apply their talents, verbally and physically, to the new experiences.

# Chronic Overthinker? Yes, That's Me!

*Delight* in exploring the details and possibilities of *all* aspects of a question, problem, or situation.

Part of the learning style is a *need* to know *all* the reasons or details of a project.

Literal *thinking* and *communicating* is of extreme importance.

So obsessed with a thought, that important tasks are not completed.

*Every* conversation is material for a verbal analysis and discussion.

Knowing and saying the *right answer* is often more important than the social costs of interrupting or correcting others.

Tendency to *correct authority figures* and peers if their details are perceived as not 100% accurate.

Participating in recreational non-intellectual pursuits *gets in the way* of thinking or researching.

# Managing the Inside of My Overthinking Mind

Realize the world often places *limits on intelligible input.*

Conformity can reduce stress and create a *future environment* to respectfully add creative insights.

Knowing many interesting answers to a question is a gift. *Give the most common first.* Save the others for another time.

Run from *"analysis paralysis"* in constantly looking for additional possibilities. Embrace one answer and move on.

Physically *change an environment* and seek other senses to shake the overthinking thoughts.

Look for *practical distractions* from the thought. Make it a purposeful activity to jump into another subject or thought.

*Write down deadlines* with time stamps for the completion of the parts of a project. This practice will reset the mind to focus on the next part.

*Reassuring self-talk* that there is time to learn more about this subject *in the future.*

Look at the subject from a mountain-top view. *Pulling away from the details* at ground level often shakes the trance of overthinking.

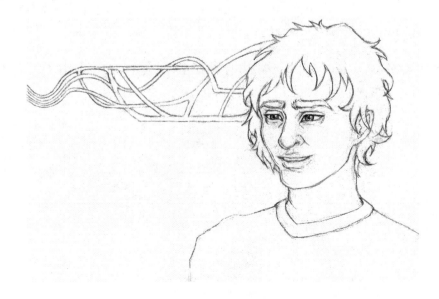

# I Have Multiple Exceptionalities (Twice Exceptional /2e)

A term used to describe a student that is *identified as gifted and has a disability.*

"If I am so good at _____, why can't I do _____?" Fill in the blanks with different activities.

There is an *exceptional ability in one area* and a perceived inability in a different area.

*Low self-esteem* is an enemy created by losing confidence in abilities and not trying something new.

*Developmental challenges* are often accompanied by high intelligence.

Organizational skills and time management skills are often lacking and may *negatively affect schoolwork.*

*Successful in one area,* such as math, drawing, verbal communication, or music.

*Significant gaps between performance* in schoolwork and performance on tests.

*Perfectionism is an enemy* and creates frustration when self-made expectations are not met.

*Twice Exceptional (2e) and dual exceptionalities* are interchangeable terms.

Watch out for "negative coping," which occurs when a Smart Kid selects an easier path to success that can be self-destructive.

Smart Kids are good at masking learning problems by using their strengths to compensate for their weaknesses.

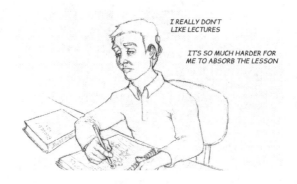

I REALLY DON'T LIKE LECTURES

IT'S SO MUCH HARDER FOR ME TO ABSORB THE LESSON

# 2e Is Powerful!

Empower a child by helping them *notice and understand* their strengths and their weaknesses.

*Identify* and *celebrate* strengths, then focus on improving weaknesses.

Keep the lines of communication open with specific praise and encouragement.

Allow the use of *preferred learning styles* for personal success (spatial, kinesthetic, auditory, visual, etc.).

Fight the frustration of not excelling in all subjects by *celebrating successes* in the best subjects.

*Look for the disconnects* between activities and results. Check out the amount of time and energy spent studying as related to the completed assignment or test grade.

*Active parents and advocates* play a key role in driving the recognition of 2e.

Prioritize training and providing positive examples in social emotional skills development: relationships, motivation, self-efficacy, and goal setting.

Extra-curricular activities benefit 2e students by pursuing *strengths*, enjoying *success,* and helping to build *confidence*.

I PREFER THE HANDS ON STUFF

# Resources and References for Further Study

Mofield, E. L. & Chakraborti-Ghosh, S. (2010). *Addressing multidimensional perfectionism in gifted adolescents with affective curriculum.* Journal for the Education of the Gifted, *33(4), 479–513. doi:10.1177/016235321003300403*

Neff, K. (2015). Self compassion: Stop beating yourself up and leave insecurity behind. *Yellow Kite.*

Neihart, M., Pfeiffer, S. I., & Cross, T. L. (2016). The social and emotional development of gifted children what do we know? *Prufrock Press Inc.*

Renzulli, J. & Reis, S. M. (2016). Reflections on gifted education: Critical works by Joseph S. Renzulli and Colleagues. *Prufrock Press.*

Rimm, S. (2008). Why bright kids get poor grades, and what you can do about it. A six-step program for parents and teachers. *Great Potential Press.*

Silverman, L. K. (2020). Giftedness 101. *Springer.*

Small, B. K. (forthcoming, March 2022). Serving the needs of your smart kids: How school leaders create a supportive school culture for the advanced learner. *Gifted Unlimited. https://www.leadsmarteducation.com.*

Terman, L. M. (1926). Genetic studies of genius. *Stanford University Press.*

Whitney, C. S. & Hirsch, G. (2007). A love for learning: Motivation and the gifted child. *Great Potential Press, Inc.*

### Websites

Davidson Institute. Gifted friendships: Age mate vs. true peer. (May 6). *http://www. davidsongifted.org/gifted-blog/gifted-friendships-age-mate-vs-true-peer/.*

Goerss, J. (2011). Asynchronous development. *SENG. (September 13).
http://www.sengifted.org/post/asynchronous-development.*

Grandell, R. (2016). Self-compassion and giftedness. *(March 22). https://
intergifted.com/wp-content/uploads/2016/03/Self-Compassion-and-
Giftedness-Handout-1.pdf.*

National Association for Gifted Children (2020) Gifted by state. *https://www.nagc.
org/gifted-state.*

National Association for Gifted Children (n.d.) Parenting for high potential.
*(Quarterly magazine). http://www.nagc.org/parenting-high-potential-1.*

National Association for Gifted Children (n.d.). Supporting twice-exceptional
students. *http://www.nagc.org/supporting-twice-exceptional-students.*

National Association for Gifted Children (n.d.) Underachievement.
*https://www.nagc.org/resources-publications/resources/
achievement-keeping-your-child-challenged/underachievement.*

Rovero, L. (2012). Many ages at once. Psychology Today. *(January 24).
http://www.psychologytoday.com/us/blog/creative-synthesis/201201/
many-ages-once.*

Trépanier, C. (2015). Yes, my gifted child is a know-it-all: A case for acceleration.
*(September 17). Crushing Tall Poppies. https://crushingtallpoppies.
com/2015/09/17/yes-my-gifted-child-is-a-know-it-all-a-case-for-acceleration/.*

## Chapter 3

# Smart Kid Social Terminology

Terms that impact the Smart Kid's social experiences in their family, school, & community

DOI: 10.4324/9781003257103 - 3

# Isolation by Choice

"I don't fit in so it's easier to be alone."

Parents often compare their Smart Kid to others their age who enjoy socializing with friends after school and on the weekends.

A child may not be happy when alone. This response may magnify unhealthy thoughts.

It is likely that some isolated children consider their computer to be their best friend.

Being alone can be a recharge time. These habits of choosing to be alone too often are difficult to break.

Isolation is comfortable for Smart Kids who may feel like misfits. Alone helps them be themselves.

Talking with peers can sometimes be a struggle or uncomfortable. There may be little joy in conversations.

Peers of the same age may not share an intellectual understanding of the subject or the world, which makes it difficult to socialize.

A child may feel as if no one understands them, so being alone avoids trying to explain themselves.

# Is Isolation Normal?

"I like being by myself. Leave me alone and don't overthink this."

Be aware of a change in routine with a need to withdraw from friends and family.

Maintain regular and consistent communication with the isolated child. Delve into why they want to be alone.

Talk with them about their perceived problems. Walk through scenarios and problem-solving ideas.

Encourage peer activities after listening to the child's opinion on their possible interests.

Investigate possible sources of emotional stress and be alert to negative social clues.

Self-destructive behaviors, eating disorders or a change in sleeping patterns are signs of distress. Investigate the reasons for these changes and give support. Seek professional counseling if appropriate.

Too much technology. Become educated about possible symptoms of internet addiction.

Find groups of like-minded children. Look outside the common age group and shift the focus to common interests.

"Being an introvert is not a bad thing. It gives me the time and space to really think."

"There are times when I am really into something and all I want to do is study and explore it for days and weeks. This does not involve other people, just me and my enthusiasm to learn."

# I Am the Best, Why Try Harder?

The student is a part of a group of regular, non-high achieving students and defined as the highest achieving member.

Adopts a "this is good enough to be the best" attitude.

Has succeeded in consistently ranking as the top student in class. This success is an expectation of others and themselves.

Definitely could meet the demands of higher rigor. But why bother?

Receives near perfect or perfect scores on all assignments easily with little effort.

Teachers consistently use this student as a positive example for others to follow.

This Smart Kid may try not to draw attention to themselves and avoids being called on in class.

Does not understand why others don't achieve like them.

Frequently is described as the "smartest kid in class."

I'M THE BEST IN THE CLASS

I DON'T FEEL THE NEED
TO PUT IN MORE EFFORT

WHAT'S THE POINT?
I DON"T GET ANYTHING ELSE
OUT OF IT

# Welcome to the Frog Pond

Achieving only enough to be at the top of the class and no more, regardless of the ability. This is referred to as Frog Pond Theory. The Smart Kid is the smartest frog in their pond. Why try to do better?

The drive to excel beyond the highest achiever in the group takes internal motivation.

It is critical to have accountability to authority figures for achieving higher goals than the other group members can achieve.

The student knows they can achieve higher standards. Gentle and constant encouragement from leaders and parents leads to a quest for reaching a higher achievement.

Goals set beyond the capacity of group members are essential to break out of the "Frog Pond."

Recognize the Smart Kid could do more. Provide accelerated content and support.

Strive to create a safe group environment for a student to excel beyond the others without ridicule or negative social pressure.

Parents and teachers explore and participate in accelerated activities in and outside the classroom.

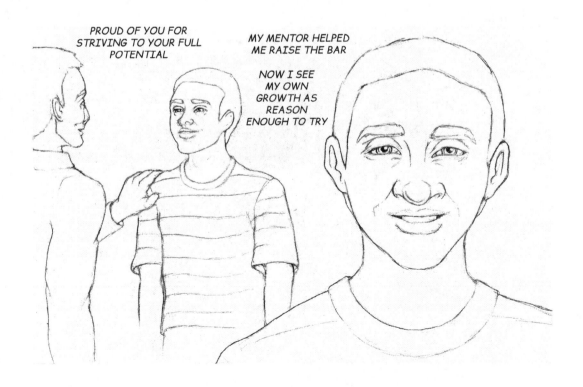

PROUD OF YOU FOR STRIVING TO YOUR FULL POTENTIAL

MY MENTOR HELPED ME RAISE THE BAR

NOW I SEE MY OWN GROWTH AS REASON ENOUGH TO TRY

# I Am Bored at School

The student has an ability to quickly grasp the depth of a lesson.

Boredom leads to frustration and can then lead to anger and anxiety.

The gifted brain is wired for complexity and a need for rigor.

The enthusiasm for learning is noticed as it starts to leave the Smart Kid.

Disengagement from school may lead to other more interesting and less appropriate stimulation.

The level of lesson delivery is not differentiated. The lesson is taught for the masses without accelerated components to stretch the gifted mind.

Staying "off the radar" is easy in the back of the class. Learning on their own is often preferred.

Frustration occurs when given busy work as a tool for killing time until the other students catch up.

Answering every question in class is often shunned by peers and teachers, leading to withdrawal.

Internalizing boredom manifests in shyness, withdrawal from activities, and even physical ailments.

# Managing Boredom

Flexible and engaging lessons built at the student's intellectual level.

Seek teachers and opportunities allowing collaboration that propel the learning experiences above the current group thinking abilities.

Families are a safe place to express boredom. Listen with interest and provide solutions with constant emotional support.

Parents take the school topics and assist in delving deeper with field trips and other exciting activities. Include friends!

Seek support from gifted teachers and school staff for ideas on accelerations in the school, classroom, and community.

Bring in the troops: gather like-minded students and provide experiences such as museums, clubs, and other stimulating activities.

*NOTHING LIKE A GOOD CHALLENGE, THANK YOU CHESS CLUB!*

# I Will Not Try That...Ever!

There is an attitude that claims there is no understanding of why trying is important.

The Smart Kid is successful in different areas. They may want to stick to what they excel in and forgo challenges.

An attempt at a new skill is daunting to the Smart Kid perfectionist who is expected to succeed at everything.

Risking ridicule for failing in a new skill or subject is not worth it.

There is a habit of not trying something new. "That is not me, it is not what I do."

The only reward for trying may be the knowledge that they tried. That may not be enough motivation to try.

The task may not be important to the Smart Kid. It may only be important to others.

There is a feeling of being trapped into trying something. This pressure is perceived as not fair.

The Smart Kid may not have the social need to please those who are encouraging them to try.

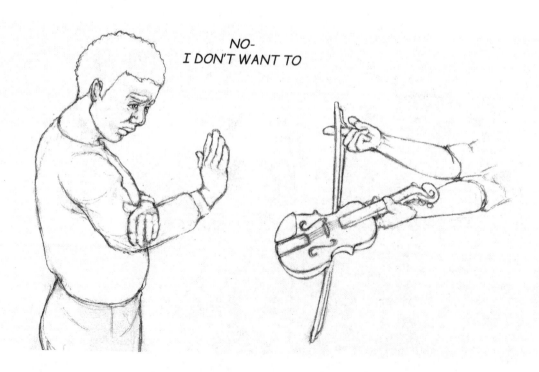

NO-
I DON'T WANT TO

# Encouragement to Give It a Try

Remind the Smart Kid about the sense of pride earned through trying something challenging and new.

Avoid punishing a student for not trying. This leads to resentment and not a change in behavior.

Listen to the reasons for not trying. They will reveal even more about the student's inner thoughts.

Break down the activity into manageable parts and support the student one part at a time.

Recollect and relate similar activities that were completed successfully.

Reflect on the reason why the child is asked to try this task. Is it really that important?

Be ready for a "fight or flight" response from the child. Predict how to encourage the activity before the child is given an opportunity to flee.

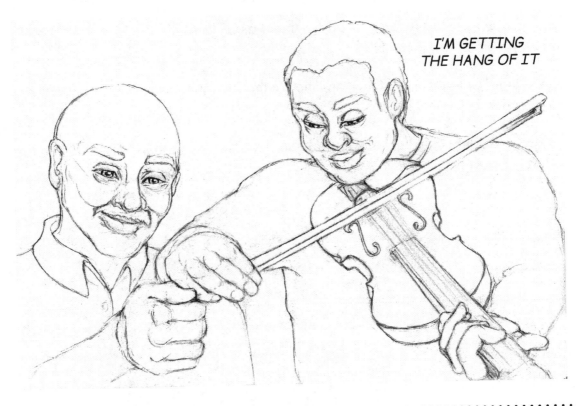

I'M GETTING THE HANG OF IT

# I Already Know ALL This Stuff!

"I just want to learn something new."

Feel irritation when others cannot remember this subject was covered in elementary school.

A reputation of knowing the right answer causes the teacher to "*always* call on someone else" when she used to be encouraged to respond in class at the beginning of the school year.

Compelled to call out answers in class regardless of the obvious irritation of class members.

A tendency to allow their minds to wander in class. Regardless, they are able to make good grades.

Working in groups to solve problems together gives opportunities to share what they already know and find new knowledge together.

"Why do I have to be in this stupid kid class?"

Class textbooks may not have current information. The Smart Kid may feel the need to point out the discrepancies to the class and teacher.

May be so engrossed in their favorite subject as a distraction in class that they fail the current class assignments.

Feels obligated to let the teacher or other authority figure know the reasons they are wrong.

"I told my teacher I could explain these math problems better than her to the class."

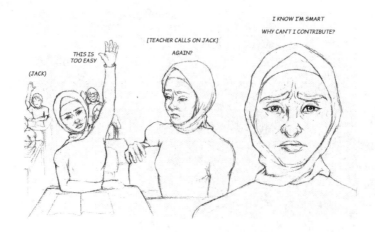

# Working with a Smart Kid

"I want to know it all. That does not make me a 'know it all'."

Realize the student is understanding at an accelerated rate and encourage their communication about their experiences in class and at home.

Listen to the Smart Kid's frustrations and provide socially acceptable problem-solving techniques.

Provide alternative responses when they know all the answers in class.

Smart Kids thrive on rigor. Introduce new subjects and work within their unique skill sets to encourage deep study and understanding inside and outside their classrooms.

Seek accelerated placement into an honors level, gifted, a higher grade, Advanced Placement, or other accelerated option. Don't give up. Keep asking the school to make accommodations.

Focus on learning how to learn, not simply learning how to study. There is a difference.

Be aware of the trap of not learning how to learn. Delve into acceleration strategies that can be applied across all subjects and situations.

Teachers adapt individual learning and allow the student to be "off task" and read on their own during lectures. Their grades will reveal if this strategy is working.

Teachers provide different and accelerated assignments, not more additional classwork.

AHH... ADVANCED WORK!
I LIKE THESE TYPES OF
CHALLENGES

# Cheaters and Liars

"Everyone else is doing it so why can't I do it too?"

Tendencies toward perfectionism often cause a social and emotional need to cheat.

Time constraints in meeting the high expectations of others force a high achiever to take drastic steps to succeed.

Placing unrealistic expectations on a Smart Kid may be perceived as forcing them to cheat.

An internal judgement after cheating or lying to succeed may lead to imposter syndrome and depression.

High achieving peers are quick to turn in known cheaters, especially after they completed their own work honestly.

Once caught cheating or lying, the reputation with teachers, parents, and students is compromised.

The risk of getting caught is overridden by the quest for the top grade.

Applying advanced intelligence to find ways to use information and technology to take unethical or illegal short cuts.

Be aware that schools made up of high achievers may have a clandestine culture of cheating. Social pressures in these environments make cheating normal and expected.

THIS GRADE IS WAY TOO IMPORTANT,
I CAN'T RISK DOING POORLY...

I'M SURE SHE HAS THE
RIGHT ANSWERS

# Taking the High Road

Teamwork is not cheating if collaboration is present and transparent. Collusion is cheating, not collaboration. Know the difference.

Teachers create lessons on academic integrity and ethics each semester or as often as needed.

Cheating catches up to a person when similar subjects are covered and tested in higher grades or in college.

Teach that it is honorable to build an academic reputation only through excelling in one's own achievements.

Encourage the belief that an ethical choice has the highest long-term reward.

Confide in a parent or teacher the temptation to cheat. Talk it out. Seek support to do what is right.

Competition breeds temptation to take dishonest measures to succeed. Recognize these thoughts and rationalize the right path is the best path.

Avoid the trap of experiencing cheating as a dangerous thrill.

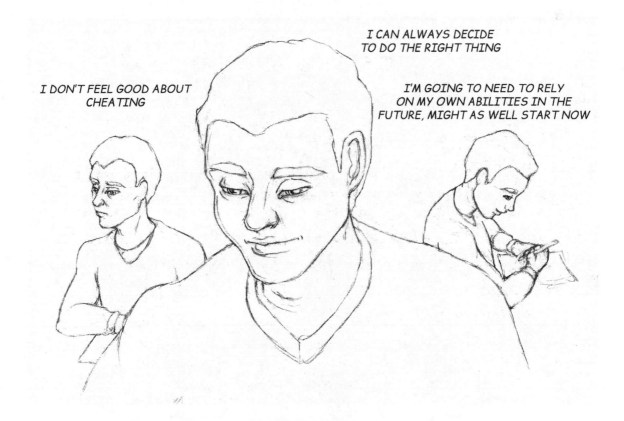

# No One Is Like Me...

Being the Smart Kid in class often makes it difficult to fit in and make friends.

There are noticeable developmental differences between the high achievers and their peers.

Parents may feel high levels of frustration and even confusion in their quest to socialize their high achieving children.

Most classrooms are filled with students who are intellectually and developmentally different from the Smart Kid.

Making friends is a sensitive and important part of childhood. The significance cannot be overemphasized for all children.

"My school doesn't have advanced classes for kids like me."

Self-isolation can lead to negative self-talk, low self-esteem, and depression.

Frustration occurs when Smart Kids develop unrealistic expectations of others. Conflicts may arise quickly between peers and authority figures.

Parents and school staff often compare the Smart Kid to siblings who may have had better social skills and made friends quickly.

I JUST DON'T RELATE TO THEM

# Find YOUR People!

Birds of a feather flock together.

Accept that an advanced learner will not be friends with every student their age. Smart Kids often prefer the companionship of older children and adults.

Parents and siblings can teach and model how to make friends.

Peers with similar interests and high intellectual complexity make the best companions regardless of their age. The number of friends is not as important as the quality of a few friends.

Be alert and listen; notice emotional and behavioral changes, which could indicate bullying.

Find the places where similar people gather. Is it a school for high achievers? The chess or robotics club? An afterschool group for Smart Kids?

Give *Smart Kid Terminology* to administrators and other personnel responsible for scheduling students. This resource encourages grouping students appropriately.

Look for enrichment with true peers in summer programs. These new friendships will continue throughout the school year. If a community cannot be found, grow one!

Not all Smart Kids have a parent support system. Teachers and counselors are critical in finding supports and grouping students appropriately.

Parents make it easy for their child to get together with friends outside of school. Be flexible and available.

Parents allow children to make friends on their own without judgment.

WE'RE ALL IN DIFFERENT GRADES,
BUT WE LOVE THE SAME THINGS

# High Expectations of Others

Placement in classes of students with lesser abilities triggers frustration, isolation, and tendency to misbehave or withdraw.

High expectations of others arise from their own pressure to excel from parents, peers, and teachers.

Criticism of others for not achieving is based on a child's cognitive understanding of their own abilities. This understanding may or may not be accurate.

It is possible that the Smart Kid does not understand others are incapable of their level of understanding. Empathy may not be present when experiencing this frustration.

A high-achieving student feels different from others who they see as not behaving, speaking, or learning like they learn.

Outward criticism of others may be a signal to parents and teachers that the Smart Kid is looking for high achievers like themselves.

There is a search for self-identity that occurs when a comparison of their own intellectual development is made with their peers.

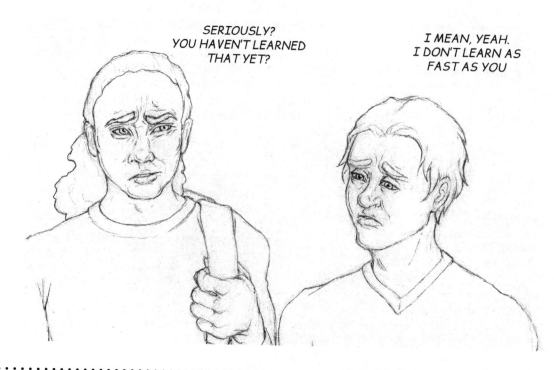

# Managing Expectations

Discuss openly how others have a different and equally valuable mindset, experience, and opinion.

Provide a toolkit of social skills to use when others are perceived as not meeting a Smart Kid's expectations.

The high expectations of others in childhood can be a trait that leads to being a successful adult.

Encourage a child to recognize, and even list, the assets of a person they perceive as not meeting their expectations. Build empathy for others.

Recognize others may not be developing at the same rate intellectually. Encourage patience and friendships.

Seek out peers with a similar intellectual capacity. True peers may not be the same age or grade.

*Find Your People!* Seek out intellectually, emotionally, and artistically similar peers.

Encourage and model the acceptance of common interests and not the differences of others.

Discuss empathy and how it applies to diverse persons and daily situations.

HEY, I'M SORRY
WE DON'T NEED TO COMPARE

YOUR VALUE GOES
WAY BEYOND THIS

THANKS, MAN

# Does Gifted Always Mean Smart?

"They say I am *Gifted*; does that mean I am Smart? Maybe, I don't want to be a Smart Kid."

"I am good at some things, but I struggle in other things. Am I still gifted?"

The high expectations for advanced performance in all attempts induce stress. There may be a tendency to hide giftedness to avoid performance pressure.

"Now that I am identified as 'gifted', do I have to change my friends?"

Being identified as gifted may make a student feel different from longtime friends.

There may be an exclusion from fun activities, such as recess, for "gifted pullouts."

"Why do all the adults want me to be gifted? What do they get out of it?"

In a group of 30 children, there are diverse learners with exceptional abilities in different areas. Some were screened and identified as gifted. Others were not given the opportunity to be assessed and are not identified as gifted. How different are they?

# Gifted Is Only One Measure of a Person

"Gifted" is an assessment-based analysis of a person's brain and how it reasons. This screening generally takes place one time early in the school experience.

Screenings or assessments may be limited to analyzing the student's acumen in specific areas. Other areas of achievement may not be assessed.

Fitting in with peers may be more important to a Smart Kid than being served by schools as a gifted student.

Students identified as gifted are encouraged to honor this difference with pride while seeking opportunities to meet similar individuals and continue growing in their giftedness.

Encourage communication if a gifted student is choosing to hide or downplay their giftedness. Listen to their reasons. Provide support and opportunities to excel where and when they are comfortable.

Give students identified as gifted a choice in their "gifted" activities.

Encourage enrichment outside of school and peer groups. Take family outings to museums, planetariums, libraries, and dinosaur digs. Give opportunities to explore in the area of giftedness at home with robotic kits, college textbooks, science experiments, written debates, or volunteering for a personal cause.

THERE'S NOT ONE WAY TO BE GIFTED

# Resources and References for Further Study

Galbraith, J. & Delisle, J. R. (2015). When gifted kids don't have all the answers: How to meet their social and emotional needs. *Free Spirit Publishing.*

Isaacson, K. L. J. (2007). Life in the fast brain. *Great Potential Press.*

Neff, K. (2015). Self compassion: Stop beating yourself up and leave insecurity behind. *Yellow Kite.*

Olszewski-Kubilius, P. & Limburg-Weber, L. (1999). Options for middle school and secondary level gifted students. Journal for the Education of the Gifted. doi:10.4219/jeg-1999–564

Peters, D. B. (2014). From worrier to warrior: A guide to conquering your fears. *Great Potential Press, Inc.*

Roedell, W. C. (1984). Vulnerabilities of highly gifted children. Roeper Review, 6(3), 127–130. doi:10.1080/02783198409552782

Winner, E. (2000). The origins and ends of giftedness. American Psychologist, 55(1), 159–169. doi:10.1037/0003–066x.55.1.159

## Websites

Byrdseed. (n.d.). Lessons that get kids' brains sweating! *https://www.byrdseed.com/.*

Davidson Institute (2020). Disproving myths about gifted students. (December 4). *https://www.davidsongifted.org/gifted-blog/disproving-myths-about-gifted-students/.*

Emamzadeh, A. (2021). Self-esteem and the frog-pond effect. Psychology Today. (July 8). *https://www.psychologytoday.com/us/blog/finding-new-home/202107/self-esteem-and-the-frog-pond-effect.*

*Institute for Educational Advancement (2014). Friendship and the gifted child. Blog post (January 8).* https://educationaladvancement.wordpress. com/2014/08/01/friendship-and-the-gifted-child/.

*Mula, K. A., Janus, P., & Palomar, D. (n.d.) Gifted children and social relationships. Afg Guidance Center.* https://afgfamily.com/blog/gifted-children/gifted-children-and-social-relationships/.

*National Association for Gifted Children (n.d.) Traits of giftedness.* https://www. nagc.org/resources-publications/resources/my-child-gifted/ common-characteristics-gifted-individuals/traits.

*Post, Dr. G. (2016). Is your gifted teen socially isolated?* https://giftedchallenges. blogspot.com/2016/08/is-you-gifted-teen-socially-isolated.html.

*Weir, K. (2013). Feel like a fraud? American Psychological Association. (November)* https://www.apa.org/gradpsych/2013/11/fraud.

## Chapter 4

# Smart Kid Emotional Terminology

### Terms that impact the Smart Kid's daily emotional well-being

DOI: 10.4324/9781003257103 - 4

# I Feel Everything... Intensely!

"The feelings of all my emotions are strong and real to me!"

This intensity is often referred to as "overexcitability," defined as heightened awareness of a person's environment.

Feelings of depression can be a result of overexcitability that is not noticed or managed.

Frequently described as a "sensitive" person.

"No one gets me! Is there something wrong with how I feel?"

Experiencing all-encompassing emotions about an event or perceived unfairness.

Feelings of isolation when others do not notice or feel as intensely.

Overstimulation occurs and may manifest into fears, anxiety, and even phobias.

Outwardly upset about world events, moral issues, and social justice.

Experiences a vivid imagination of what could or has already happened.

Sensitive and vocal about the state of the environment. Adopts a "cause" and worries about it intensely.

Feels deep compassion for others, especially outcasts.

# It's OK to Be Intense

Listen to the Smart Kid with tendencies of overexcitability. Let them talk about it.

Never try to suppress a feeling or keep a child from communicating their anxiety, fears, or emotions.

Notice the intense emotion is happening. It's here. Feel it. Recognize the intensity for what it is.

Feel the emotion as it is occurring and experience it in a socially acceptable way without fear of judgement from others.

Voice concerns and thoughts openly in a safe place to let go of emotional steam.

Compassion from friends, family, and school staff is essential in managing and communicating emotions.

Build relationships with those of similar interests and intensities both in and outside the peer group.

Accept that personal emotions are more pronounced than others.

Self-reflect on each emotional situation and seek counsel from trusted peers or authority figures.

Stay away from "just relax, it's not that bad" dialogues. Suppressing concerns may lead to anxiety or depression.

Be aware of and avoid harmful people who try to make the intense child feel inferior or ashamed of how they feel.

LEARNING TO PROCESS AND EXPRESS MY
EMOTIONS HAS HELPED ME NAVIGATE THEM

# Imposter Syndrome

"I feel like a fraud. I should not be here. They are going to find out I don't know this stuff."

Experiencing a real sense of intellectual self-doubt.

Doubting they have the ability to succeed in a new environment.

Possibly occurring due to a manifestation of the external pressures to be advanced in all subjects.

Real feelings of inadequacy that they do not belong in their current position or situation.

Students of diversity may experience intense feelings that they do not belong. Especially if they are unique when compared to their classmates or group.

This syndrome occurs most often when a child is trying something new and different. Insecurities in their abilities are rationalized and turned into a fear to try.

The Smart Kid may attribute successes to having good luck or being at the "right place at the right time."

Most will suffer in silence for fear others will unmask their perceived lack of abilities.

This syndrome occurs with perfectionists and may lead to a heightened sensitivity and even social isolation.

# I Deserve to Be Here

Encourage the Smart Kid to talk about this syndrome with supporters who know and can articulate the student's strengths as assets and applicable to the situation.

Explain that new endeavors are a challenge not a threat.

Help the student embrace their differences, and the potential to not master every task, every time.

Teach interpersonal skills in recognizing personal progress and growth.

Do not assume the student will be cured after a small success. Keep up the support and encouragement.

*Accept* that a student's high intellectual complexity is paired with an emotional depth related to this syndrome.

Seek to reframe how achievements are valued. It's OK not to win, if it was fun or valuable in other aspects.

*Listen* to the student's concerns with interest and support.

# I Am So Sensitive All the Time!

"Why do I feel everything so personally?"

This sensitive Smart Kid has difficulty ignoring negative actions or words as easily as others.

Feels misunderstood by peers, parents, and teachers.

Quickly and intensely responds to negative situations as if the world is about to end.

There is a physical manifestation of feelings as heart racing or sweating when a perceived injustice occurs.

Parents, teachers, and peers will voice their irritation by telling them they are overreacting.

Insists that they are not being melodramatic. These thoughts and feelings are real.

Peers may tease and tell them they are taking a situation too seriously. This occurrence may compound sensitive feelings.

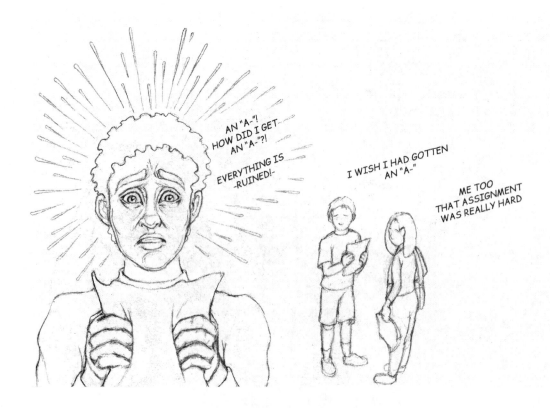

# Manage Heightened Sensitivity Naturally

Talk about how they feel about the event. Walk through each step as they describe their emotions and concerns.

Start a communication scale that reflects the intensity of the emotion. Ask the Smart Kid to scale their emotion from 1 to 10. Is the intensity a 2 or a 9?

Talk about the worst thing that could happen in an intense situation. Relieve the anxiety by describing how the parent, teacher, or peer reacts. Keep it positive.

Find a mentor who will be open to being the person the child goes to for an appraisal of a situation as critical or not critical. This mentor could be a teacher, coach, peer, or parent who is a patient listener.

Review the outside influences on the Smart Kid. Are there people relating untrue or exaggerated negative and fearful conversations?

Teach and embed social and emotional skills in the student's daily routine. Teach them how to question a situation and take specific actions or steps to discern if it is a critical issue.

Uncover and communicate the bigger picture to the issue and how it is affected by the social, emotional, or political environment.

Recognize that young boys and certain cultures may struggle with the social and family pressures of not showing emotions.

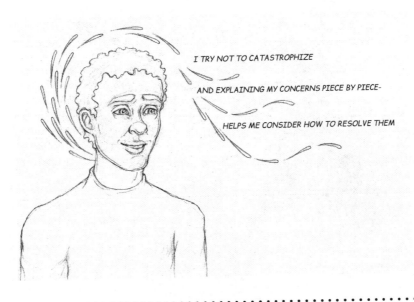

*I TRY NOT TO CATASTROPHIZE*

*AND EXPLAINING MY CONCERNS PIECE BY PIECE-*

*HELPS ME CONSIDER HOW TO RESOLVE THEM*

# I Have a Strong Sense of Justice!

The "righter of wrongs" and the seeker of truth.

Adopts a "cause" and worries about it intensely and openly.

Does not understand why others do not see the injustice for their cause.

This Smart Kid enthusiastically seeks fairness for all people.

Compassionate for others, especially outcasts, and protective of all people, creatures, and the planet.

Empathetic with a deep capacity for caring that is often described as stubborn, but well-informed.

Communicates their rational with a clear definition of ethics and "what is the right thing to do."

Outwardly upset when a class member is treated unfairly or humiliated.

Frustrated that others may see shades of gray areas when truth and justice must prevail.

There is no tolerance for systems that stand in the way of their belief in justice.

High moral reasoning comes with the complexity of thought that relates the truth, even when it hurts themselves or others.

# Negotiating the "It's Not Fair" Attitude

Reveal the bigger picture of the issue and talk openly about how it is affected by the social, emotional, or political environment.

Recognize and support the strong belief that a situation is unethical. Then, work together to break it down to determine the best reaction in public or personally.

The perception of justice may change with maturity. Watch, listen, and support these changes as they develop through the Smart Kid's youth and adulthood.

Patiently explain how historical systems are created with barriers to the perceived injustice before relating the steps on how to change systems.

Change a "strong sense of justice" to a "development of robust morals and helpful habits."

Create a safe communication system when a rigid notion of fairness arises. Teach the skills to see all sides of an issue and use them repeatedly.

Explore organizations and clubs that support the child's passion. Get involved as a class or a family.

Encourage leadership opportunities in their passion.

Stay away from "life is not fair" dialogues. The passionate Smart Kid will not accept this concept.

# Feeling Down and Depressed

"I am here. Look at me. Don't you notice that there is a dark cloud in my world?"

Unmet and unrealistic expectations of self have the capacity to generate sadness and despair.

The problems of an advanced learner are frequently ignored because they are not troublemakers, and they are perceived as having it all together.

Tendencies toward sensitivity and social isolation are often misdiagnosed as depression.

Frustration and anger may be generated through not having the power to change an unfair situation.

The Smart Kid may have the emotionally intense perception that they are misunderstood and not noticed as being special by parents, peers, or teachers.

Advanced intelligence can be stressful when critical judgements are applied to self and others.

Parents may feel and express a heightened sense of anxiety as they struggle to meet the needs of their high achieving children.

Depression is often first noticed as it manifests into physical ailments such as stomach aches, nausea, acne, and blushing.

A depressed gifted child can be a master at "staying off the radar" of family and school personnel.

I FEEL SO ALONE

NO ONE UNDERSTANDS

# Managing the Blues

Accept that a child's high intellectual complexity is paired with an equally intense emotional depth.

Teach risk resiliencies through practical conversations and real-life scenarios of concern in the student's life.

Parents allow children to be themselves without judgement or strict rules and schedules.

Provide positive experiences for the child on a predictable basis throughout their week.

Listen to the student's concerns with interest and support.

"Talking it out" is a technique used to deescalate a depressive state. Listen, do not always give a solution, simply be present for the talk.

Don't assume your child doesn't need your attention or intervention because they are doing well in school.

Be alert, look out for emotional and physical indications a child needs professional counseling.

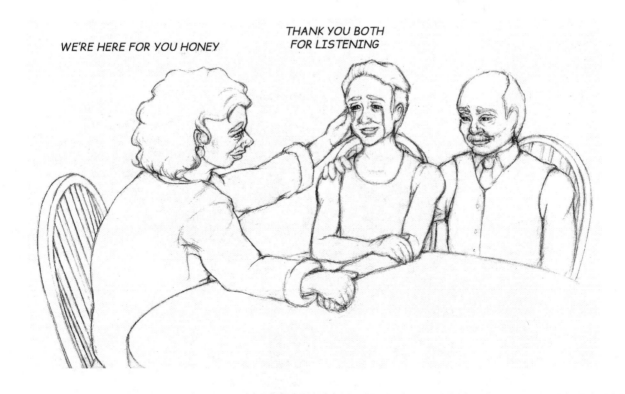

WE'RE HERE FOR YOU HONEY

THANK YOU BOTH FOR LISTENING

# Stress Is a Monster

"Life's stressors are like big mean monsters that take over my brain."

There is a clear and present belief that anything less than perfect is a failure.

The Smart Kid's feeling that there is a social competition to know and be the smartest is a real and authentic belief.

Stress occurs when a student knows they are not good at a task or activity. They worry about letting the people down who believe they can do everything at an advanced level.

Invisible and self-imposed higher and higher standards drive daily stress.

Stress is noticed in personality changes such as irritability, worrying, negative temperaments, attitudes, and a lack of enthusiasm.

Stress is caused by the perception that parents, peers, and teachers all have expectations of them to be better and smarter than all others.

Experiencing the world with more intensity leads to a heightened sense of anxiety and depression.

Stress can be manifested in physical ways, such as a change in sleep patterns, a separation from peers, and less personal grooming.

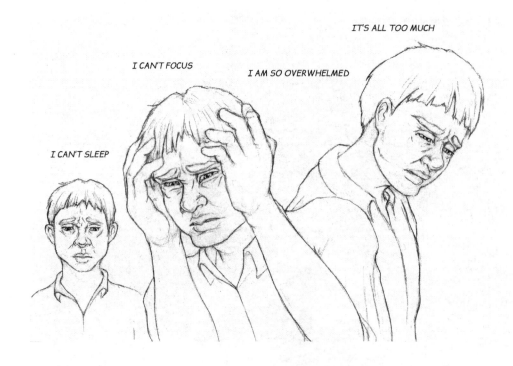

# Working the Stress Out of a Smart Kid

Recognize that stress occurs internally. This is a mindset. Identify the feeling. Acknowledge its power.

Understand that a child's inner voice is louder than a peer or family member's compassionate and rational argument against the stressor.

Search for and apply age- and intelligence-related stress management skills directly related to a child's personal stressors. First step: identify the stressors. Second step: give tools for management.

Make lists and cross out what is completed. Put time stamps by each item on the list. This action helps the Smart Kid feel productive and accomplished.

Writing down worries will take the edge off their power. Journaling is a liberating exercise in self-acknowledgment and discovery.

Verbally walk through the stressor and talk about how it will not be as negative as perceived. Stay positive and encouraging.

Protect a child's environment from distractions when big projects are due. Be an encouraging partner and not a disciplinarian.

IT'S BEEN A HUGE RELIEF; LEARNING TO STRUCTURE MY SCHEDULE-

AND FINDING AN OUTLET FOR MY NEGATIVE THOUGHTS

# I'm Not Good at Anything

Often, these are the feelings of an asynchronous learner who is a master at some subjects and not others.

Tend to not live up to their own expectations due to identifying what they are good at as compared to others.

A gap in understanding why they excel at some subjects, yet do not understand or relate to others.

The Smart Kid may be confused by the identification of their true talents. No one has ever helped them.

Failure is the only outcome outside of perfection.

Makes a critical observation of others achieving higher success in seemingly easy activities.

There is a fear of falling into mediocrity in any subject and losing their ability to be a successful perfectionist.

The feeling of being an outsider is magnified when success is not achieved as quickly as expected by themselves or others.

Past failures leach into thoughts and cause the feelings of shame and unworthiness.

Anxiety starts physically and mentally when thinking of a past failure.

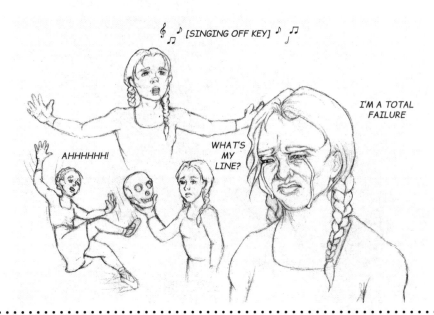

# Managing Self-criticism

Teach the child to recognize and acknowledge their own self-criticism.

Focus conversations about positive traits and experiences prior to talking about more challenging situations.

Develop a daily habit of encouraging self-compassion through actions and words.

Ask the child to repeat their positive traits. Walk through this mental exercise daily.

Learn to predict a Smart Kid's reaction when exposed to a new challenge. Talk about this future experience and give tools to help the child address insecurities.

Encourage the child to verbally talk about their strengths and especially when self-criticism occurs.

Recognize that self-criticism has a power to control the mind and actions. Fight it with deliberate positive self-talk.

Assist in adapting personal standards to more manageable and obtainable standards.

# Gifted Kid Burnout

"I am tired of the high expectations everyone has of me."

It is noticed that the Smart Kind has lost an enthusiasm for learning.

Disengagement from school leads to other more interesting and unhealthy stimulations.

A student who has not been challenged in achieving good grades may have not learned how to "learn" or study effectively. When a challenge occurs, they stop trying.

Believes their success in school is the measure of their own self-worth.

Teachers expect and push the Smart Kid to continue to take high-level classes.

A difficult class may lead to a student not knowing how to proceed to get the good grade.

A good work ethic is not established because past assignments were easy.

Too much homework and the high expectations to succeed in higher grade levels lead to burnout.

The expectation to take all high-level classes is overwhelming for a Smart Kid's time and mental energy.

Pressure from parents to keep getting "A's" in all upper level classes that are exceedingly difficult and time-consuming. There is no time for fun classes.

High-achieving peer groups expect all their friends to be high-achievers and may ostracize a former member who has sliding grades.

THIS IS TOO MUCH

I'M EXHAUSTED

EVERYONE WANTS SOMETHING FROM ME

# Hang In There and Enjoy Giftedness

Talk to friends, family, and teachers about how their high expectations are frustrating and hurtful.

Predict the level of expectation of others and counter it quickly with your intentions. Be clear and concise on decisions.

Avoid the fixed mindset of having to achieve perfect grades. Let it go.

Reflect on what brings joy. Make sure these activities are part of every day.

Realize that natural talent is not always enough to get the grade. Learning how to learn gets the grade.

Look for activities that feed the creative side of the brain. Jump into them with both feet.

Seek out positive people with common interests in the same causes and activities. They are motivators.

Look outside the usual peer group for positive motivators with a unique mindset.

Stay strong with your decision to cut back on high level classes. Let everyone know you are the person who must do all the work.

Insist on being referred to as a "hard worker," not just a Smart Kid. This definition lets everyone know that keeping good grades and succeeding takes time and focused work.

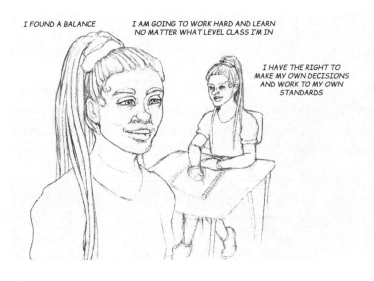

I FOUND A BALANCE    I AM GOING TO WORK HARD AND LEARN NO MATTER WHAT LEVEL CLASS I'M IN

I HAVE THE RIGHT TO MAKE MY OWN DECISIONS AND WORK TO MY OWN STANDARDS

# Resources and References for Further Study

Alias, A., Rahman, S., Majid, R. A., & Yassin, S. F. (2013). Dabrowski's overexcitabilities profile among gifted students. Asian Social Science, 9(16). doi:10.5539/ass.v9n16p120

Bishop, J. (2021). Anxiety solutions for smart kids: A parent's guide to managing stress and anxiety in gifted children. Prufrock Press.

Clance, P. R. & Imes, S. A. (1978). The imposter phenomenon in high achieving women: Dynamics and therapeutic intervention. Psychotherapy: Theory, Research & Practice, 15(3), 241–247. doi:10.1037/h0086006

Coleman, L. J. & Cross, T. L. (2005). Being gifted in school: An introduction to development, guidance, and teaching. Prufrock Press.

Daniels, S. & Piechowski, M. (eds) (2009) Living with intensity: Understanding the sensitivity, excitability, and the emotional development of gifted children, adolescents, and adults. Great Potential Press.

Small, B. K. (forthcoming, March 2022). Serving the needs of your Smart Kids: How school leaders create a supportive school culture for the advanced learner. Gifted Unlimited. https://www.leadsmarteducation.com.

Van Tassel-Baska, J. (2021). Talent development in gifted education theory, research, and practice. Routledge.

Vialle, W., Heaven, P. C., & Ciarrochi, J. (2007). On being gifted, but sad and misunderstood: Social, emotional, and academic outcomes of gifted students in the Wollongong Youth Study. Educational Research and Evaluation, 13(6), 569–586. doi:10.1080/13803610701786046

Vialle, W., Ashton, T., Carlon, G., & Rankin, F. (2001). Acceleration: A coat of many colours. Roeper Review, 24(1), 14–19. doi:10.1080/02783 190109554119

*Whitney, C. S. & Hirsch, G. (2011).* Helping gifted children soar: A practical guide for parents and teachers. *Great Potential Press.*

## Websites

*Davidson Institute (n.d.)* Resources for gifted children & their families. *https://www. davidsongifted.org.*

*Mula, K. A., Janus, P., & Palomar, D. (n.d.)* Gifted children and social relationships. *Afg Guidance Center. https://afgfamily.com/blog/gifted-children/ gifted-children-and-social-relationships/.*

*National Association for Gifted Children (n.d.).* Traits of giftedness. *https:// www.nagc.org/resources-publications/resources/my-child-gifted/ common-characteristics-gifted-individuals/traits.*

*Silverman, L. K. (n.d.).* What we have learned about gifted children. *https:// web.archive.org/web/20140216195224/http://www.gifteddevelopment. com:80/What_is_Gifted/learned.htm.*

# Chapter 5

# Smart Kid
# Terminology Resources

Exploring and sharing this resource
enhances the lives of Smart Kids
and those who know them

DOI: 10.4324/9781003257103 - 5

# Taking Action with Resources

The first time a reader picks up this book and flips through the pages there is little doubt they are searching for their own traits. As they read and enjoy the illustrations, learning takes place. They may have a conversation about how they identify with the trait and how they would manage it. Another person may have simply handed the book to a co-worker or friend with no conversation. It would only take a few minutes for the reader to find themselves within the pages.

The worst-case scenario is *Smart Kid Terminology* sits on the bookshelf.

\* \* \* \* \*

Scenario:

The students are seated in neat rows of desks. This is an advanced class so there are few behavior problems. But there is still drama. It usually starts with Brad. He sits at the back of the class far away from the teacher. She purposefully placed him there to keep his outbursts from interrupting her lessons.

Brad is identified as gifted but has failing grades and can never find his homework. His parents know about his behavior but are at a loss to manage it. The school counselor is being asked to reschedule Brad into a lower-level class. Everyone agrees Brad belongs in the advanced class. So why is he so different?

The counselor finds copies of the *Smart Kid Terminology* book to share with the teacher, parent, and Brad. They are asked to read it and bring their ideas to the upcoming conference. The conference starts with a clear understanding of Brad's traits. The strategies and illustrations are the immediate conversation. Eureka – time, and a child, are saved.

\* \* \* \* \*

The frustration of knowing that a student is not working at the top of their learning ability has been felt by most educators and families. It takes work to research the causes and experiment with strategies. If advocates participate in the exploration and have a universal understanding of the traits, success is around the corner.

As stated in Chapter 1, the *Smart Kid Terminology* book is of no benefit sitting on a shelf. Its condition should have fingerprints, dog-eared pages, sticky notes on various terms, and a list of the recipients who have checked it out. Pass the book around. Share it with the clear instructions to return it with a conversation about which traits they can relate to and what was learned from the strategies for management or coping.

Teachers keep copies in the classroom to lend out to students and parents. Students keep a copy in a backpack or bedroom. Refer to it often and share it with friends and teachers. School counselors keep several copies for use in the office and to check out to students, parents, and even teachers. School leaders review the terms prior to conferences or when speaking on the phone with a parent of a Smart Kid. Refer to the terms and their strategies as your own suggestions. Parents review the terms throughout the school years. A child's academic, social, and emotional identities change with the direction of the wind from year to year. This comforting resource brought to the table when discussing feelings and situations will start those important conversations.

# Sharing Is Caring

It is natural in self-reflective actions for a person to spend their time projecting how the terms might relate to others. "Oh, I know who that is! He is such a perfectionist!" Now is the time to embrace this action and seek out persons who would benefit from a study of these academic, social, and emotional terms.

Why would this person relate to one or more of the terms? Ensure the conversation is positive and meant to nurture strengths. An openness to analyzing the terms, reviewing the illustrations, and applying the strategies may be unproductive if there is an intrusive manner of trying to "help" the child. Leave the terms with them. This is an effective method that encourages someone to read the terms without oversight. Self-reflection takes time and privacy to explore all the nuances of each term.

The result may be a disagreement with the definition of the trait and its strategies. That is OK. The conversation has started. Delve into their opinion using the book as an example. Discuss the management of some traits and the solutions of others. Just talk about it!

# Further Study

Chapters are divided into Academic, Social, and Emotional terminology. Each chapter includes valuable resources for a further study of each term. Explore the citations to find a relatable format or content. This exercise will reveal several common resources related to multiple sections. Get to know the experts in the field. Recognize their contributions. Researchers may find that certain publications or websites appeal to their interests and needs. Use these resources for continued study of the learning and support of our Smart Kids.

Use the terms as a jumping-off point for more individualized research. There are vast amounts of information pertaining to specific traits. Understand that some sources are purely for conversations and not research-based. Others take an academic tone and format along with the credibility of independent research. Find what appeals to the reader and work diligently to learn about Smart Kids.

# About the Author

As an educator for over 20 years, Dr. Brenda Kay Small has served in schools, universities, and private businesses.

She is an advanced learner advocate, author, and presenter. Her book *Serving the Needs of Smart Kids: How School Leaders Create a Supportive School Culture for the Advanced Learner* provides schools with a pragmatic resource to create a school environment designed to support high-level learners. She uses her opportunities as a guest speaker, a presenter at multiple conferences, and an author to spread the news on how and why to build supportive cultures in student-centered environments.

Her leadership experience reaches beyond schools and into communities through the mentoring and teaching of future school leaders. She has taught masters and doctoral level education leadership courses at four different universities in two states. She enjoys the challenge of writing a contemporary and meaningful graduate level education leadership course curriculum.

She earned the Administrator of the Year Award for her work in building schoolwide career academies that prepare all levels of students for post-secondary success. As a classroom teacher, she received the Florida Social Science Teacher of the Year Award, and Florida's Excellence in Teaching Award.

Her doctorate and master's degrees were earned from the University of South Florida in Education Leadership and Policy Studies. A true westerner, Dr. Small and her family enjoy living in her home state of Colorado.

Illustrations by Ali Cushing.